The Public Speaking Project

The Ultimate Guide to Effective Public Speaking

How to Develop Confidence, Overcome Your Public Speaking Fear, Analyze Your Audience, and Deliver an Effective Speech

Kyle Faber

1

CAC Publishing
ISBN: 978-1-948489-14-0
Kyle Faber

Table of Contents

PART ONE:

The Foundations of

Public Speaking

CHAPTER 1 - INTRODUCING PUBLIC SPEAKING

In this day and age, communication is key. Having the ability to communicate well will give you the edge needed in order to stay up-to-date with this fast paced world. Being educated in public speaking will certainly help you work towards this goal.

Because of the diversity of opinions in our society, which can frequently be controversial, the need for good public speaking has increased. We, as individuals, need to voice our views in order to function well and get our point across. For thousands of years, public speaking has been crucial in constructing and protecting our culture and way of life. The effects of public speaking are massive and influence nearly all facets of our lives, like the way we think/act. In addition, it is used in court proceedings, congress, and also in the classroom.

Having said that, speaking in public can certainly be quite a challenge. For some people, it is a cause of embarrassment; and not just the average every-day person, but also to individuals of high rank, like lawyers, scholars, doctors, entrepreneurs, etc. In fact, most all individuals experience reluctance and anxiety in speaking in front of an audience. This anxiety can often be accompanied by our palms sweating, an embarrassing stutter, and knowing what we want to say but not being able to spit it out. These problems cause difficulties for the speaker, particularly in expressiveness, and also uncomfortable effects on their audience.

More than likely, you obtained this book because you are getting ready to give a speech and you are looking for some valuable tips. Or maybe, you just simply realize that there is a connection between successful people and effective public speaking. You hope that this book can help you, and it will do just that.

Technical terminologies in public speaking will be explained throughout and assist you in your growth as a great public speaker.

There are so many books on the subject of public speaking, but not many of them actually give practical help. This book intends to achieve what the other books have not by providing you with useful material.

This book gives careful thought relative to individuals who truly love to speak publicly. However, not everyone has the luxury of enough time to prepare for their speeches. In reading this information, you will learn not only to make your next speech a great one, but also to become even better with each subsequent speech. It will help you to write and provide a motivating, strong, and succinct speech of tremendously high quality. In addition, it will also answer any questions and fears of the occasional public speaker.

Aristotle said "a speaker needs three qualities – good sense, good character, and goodwill toward his hearers." Accordingly, public speaking is also about emerging speakers, and in the end, decent human beings.

Whether your speech is long or short, the same rules will always apply, such as the rule of <u>preparation</u>. Getting into the habit of preparing always makes for good speakers. Some speakers insist that they speak from "inspiration," when in reality, they have always prepared their speeches ahead of time.

CHAPTER 2 - PUBLIC SPEAKING AND YOU

Some individuals are born to be speakers. However, most just are not. Therefore, you are not alone if you sincerely don't like giving speeches and speaking in front of a big audience. For most of us, stage fright is unavoidable. Actors and actresses are almost always nervous prior to a performance.

You may believe that your career doesn't require public speaking. This is where you are incorrect, because regardless of what job you have, public speaking will eventually come into the picture, somehow, someway. Therefore, this chapter will focus on the importance of public speaking in our everyday lives and also on some of the essentials of communication procedures.

What Roles Can Public Speaking Play in Your Life?

Being successful in public speaking can be so beneficial and begin a world of opportunities in your life. A newly found love of it can assist you in conquering without limits. It will broaden your possibilities through individual development, inspiration, and progressing in your career.

1. Public Speaking Improves Your Personal Development

In Abraham Maslow's "Hierarchy of Needs", realizing your self-worth ranks the highest. Giving a speech actually aids the speaker to realize his/her self-worth via the personal satisfaction he/she experiences every time a great speech is given. You, as the speaker, will become more self-assured, particularly when the audience reacts positively. It will also decrease anxiety when requested by an expert to speak.

Think of the student who dropped a public speaking course many times because she loathed speaking in front of her class. Nonetheless, after a study on building up her self-confidence, she decided to give it a go and was extremely successful. In fact, she began to love the experience so much that she even volunteered to give more speeches.

Public speaking tools such as research, conceptualization, and organization, give you have a methodical and operational way of presenting your ideas. Hence, you will ultimately have the ability to express yourself much better. In the interim, you will likewise become more open to others. Moreover, these speaking skills will place you in a more substantial role when you speak with people of high standing. Finally, public speaking fulfills your sense of accomplishment when the onlookers accept you affectionately. This reveals your level of communication skills and intelligence. All of the above contribute greatly to your self-esteem.

2. Public Speaking Influences Your Society

Keep in mind that it is not only you who can profit from good communication skills but society also. Governments, most times, listen to the voice of their citizens. With the correct communication abilities, you can represent the public in articulating your rights and opinions.

For instance, a community discussion can be quite beneficial. Typically when any neighborhood holds regular meetings, they will discuss particular concerns and/or courses of action. During these discussions, many opinions are communicated and now you will have a clear interaction of public speaking.

All individuals need to speak in public at some point, whether ceremoniously or otherwise. This consists of kids in school, to people in a town meeting, to residents voicing issues, etc. There is honestly no way you can avoid it.

3. Public Speaking Advances Your Profession

In addition to everything above, public speaking can also assist in your occupation, and ultimately, your finances. Generally, accomplishment is measured by answers to questions like, "How long have you been in your job?" or "Do you hold a degree?" Conversely, it has been proven by researchers that the greatest meter of success in any vocation is whether the person is frequently requested to provide speeches. The individuals who tend to contribute more speeches are inclined to have greater salaries than those who give less or no speeches.

Take the average worker, for instance. She registers for a public speaking seminar which is held 2 hours a week for 6 weeks. After 2 months, she is promoted to a senior position within her company! Her boss has obviously been observing her outstanding presentations.

The more time that you work for any business, and the higher you climb within the company, the more your boss will request that you to preside over company meetings and give talks to the staff and/or the clients. The greater your position, the more responsibilities you will incur leading the individuals under you; which means the more you must speak successfully. A manager once said, "From the chairman of the board to the assistant manager of the most obscure department, nearly everyone in business speaks in public or makes a speech at some time or the other."

Apart from large establishments, such as Apple or General Motors, smaller organizations and businesses within the country also want employees who are decent public speakers. Think about the high school coach. If he/she is not convincing enough to express to the school board that new gym equipment is necessary, the school athletes may have to make due with the old equipment.

Another example would be parents who are trying to convince the school board that a school dress code is no longer necessary. If they are not good with their words, their children could end up continuing to wear uniforms in school. Salespeople are a great example also. If they can't describe their products with a substantial sales pitch, then obviously less people would tend to buy the products. This is also true for many other professions.

Wherever you may find yourself in life, you will come across occasions which require you to speak in public.

CHAPTER 3 - GETTING STARTED: YOUR FIRST SPEECH

Envision being in a classroom. Look around and try to decide who you think speaks well. You may choose someone who looks smart or someone who frequently talks in class. You might believe that these individuals are in fact more confident than you. Or perhaps you believe that they were just born speakers and you are not.

Well, you may be surprised to know that they are most likely thinking the same thing about you! They might think that you are the one who is a born speaker, and they actually envy you because they have a fear of public speaking. The bottom line is that most people do not know much at all about it.

On the other hand, you might really be a good speaker without even knowing it. You won't actually know until doing it and by seeing yourself doing it.

Take, for instance, this student during his first speech in class:

He had to organize a long speech. Two weeks prior to giving the speech, he started writing. He was so stressed that he had a hard time sleeping at night. The night prior to his speech, he did not sleep at all. Nevertheless, when he finally presented the speech and saw it on video, he recognized that it was not as bad as he anticipated it to be. By watching the video, he learned that he had essentially improved in public speaking.

You can also watch yourself speak in front of a mirror.

Preparing Yourself to Speak

Below are some basic rules of public speaking:

- ✓ **Gain an understanding of who you are**. Realize your own awareness, abilities, preferences and aptitudes.
- ✓ **Gain an understanding of your audience**. Consider what you believe the audience wants to hear, what incites their interest, what they believe in and what they want to know.
- ✓ **Gain an understanding of the situation**. Reflect upon how the setting and other unanticipated factors could have an impact on the way you deliver your speech.
- ✓ **Anticipate response from the audience**. Be sure to have a strong and clear purpose in mind so your audience will respond the way you plan.
- ✓ **Search for other sources of information**. Always search for more resources which can make your speech more vibrant.
- ✓ **Come up with an argument that is reasonable**. Be sure that the purpose of your speech is reinforced by

strong and trustworthy data in order to articulate a sound argument.

✓ **<u>Add structure to your message</u>**. Bring together your ideas so that the audience will not have a hard time following your speech.

✓ **<u>Talk directly to your audience</u>**. Be sure that the language you are using is one that your audience is comfortable with. And, always reflect upon the occasion in delivering your speech.

✓ **<u>Gain self-confidence through practice</u>**. Only practice can help you successfully present your speech. Master the flow of your performance by continually rehearsing it. Practice is what will give you command over your speech.

Becoming a Good Public Speaker

Most everyone at one time or another has listened to a professor give a boring and monotonous lecture. Many people don't give much importance to good speeches and just simply try to stick to teaching. However, these speakers are probably not aware that they are ineffective, due to the fact that they lack certain knowledge about the basic characteristics of a good speech. Therefore, to avoid this drawback, you should know and remember some of the basic principles.

1. Respect the variety of the audience.

Good speakers will never look down upon their audience. They will always consider the audience as their equals. They know that all listeners have diverse backgrounds; therefore communicating to each of them effectively as individuals would also involve diverse approaches.

Prior to organizing your speech, you must take your audience into consideration. You should consider things such as age, gender, and cultural background. What does your audience know about the topic? What are their beliefs and values? By considering these factors, you can now select a topic which suits them and prepare your speech in a way which would be most effective.

The entire experience will be much more enjoyable if you prepare your speech for the distinct and cultural differences of the audience. For instance, will both males and females be open and appreciate the material that you have prepared? Would a Hispanic audience be at ease with the language you are using as much as the Native Americans would? Would any of your comments offend senior citizens while addressing a younger generation?

The more you know about your audience, the better the chances you will get their attention and the more your speech will fit the situation.

In other words, the audience will be comfortable listening to you and you will have a better interaction with them.

2. Know as much as possible about listening.

Effective communication doesn't only depend on being a good speaker; it also depends upon having good listeners. It is definitely a two-way process. If you as the speaker prepares a refined speech, it would be ultimately be inadequate if the audience is not listening. You must also know how to read the reactions of your audience. How at ease or uncomfortable they look says volumes about their interest or understanding.

3. Organize carefully to improve understanding and recall.

The greatest demonstrations have joined ideas which run effortlessly. This is effective since the listeners are capable of following your arguments and thus will not be confused.

Three parts of a well-organized speech:
- **Introduction**: Be sure to capture the attention of your audience, increase their interest, and give them a good explanation of your topic.

- **Body**: Begin with your key ideas. Keep them structured and be sure to support them with visual and verbal aids when possible.
- **Conclusion**: Deliver a summary of your points and connect them in a way which will produce an impact, allowing them to remember your points.

4. Use language effectively.

Keep it short and simple. The simpler the language, the more commanding and thought-provoking your speech will be. Using too many words to express a single idea will confuse the audience and therefore make your argument weak and possibly boring. By keeping your presentation short but precise, they will remember what you say and appreciate it.

5. Sound natural and enthusiastic.

A natural problem with first-time speech givers is that they either memorize their speech word for word or they depend on too many flashcards as notes. Memorization and flashcards can cause the speaker to sound unnatural. Converse normally to people to make them listen better.

By being natural and eager, it seems more like chatting with your friends. Essentially, avoid trying to speak under the guise of professionalism when you talk. Treat it as though it were an everyday conversation with your friends or family.

6. Use high-quality visual aids.

A humble writing comprising of fundamental phrases and pictures is a perfect visual aid. Typically, visual aids are anything which complements your speech. It will significantly aid your audience to follow the flow of your ideas and to comprehend them quicker. It also gives believability to your speech, which will make you more relaxed and confident. On the other hand, try to avoid creating poor images, because they will become more of a distraction than anything. You must treat your visuals with the same importance as your speech itself.

7. Give only ethical speeches.

Accurateness is also vital. It would be challenging for your audience to make educated choices if the material you give is either false or even vague. Do your research in order to guarantee credibility and clarity. Do not plagiarize, falsify or exaggerate your information.

Likewise, when attempting to sway your audience one way or the other, don't manipulate, mislead, force, or pressure. Make sure you develop good arguments thru sound reasoning and solid evidence. This is called "ethical persuasion". When info is fabricated, it then becomes disreputable since it thwarts listeners from making knowledgeable choices.

Essentially, good speakers will aim to alter the views, ethics, or outlooks of their audience thru clean persuasion.

CHAPTER 4 - DEVELOPING SPEAKER CONFIDENCE

Despite how interested and/or experienced we might be in public speaking, something that usually can't be avoided is anxiety, particularly when the day of the speech gets closer. We ask ourselves questions which usually makes our stomachs turn. You'll be thinking: Will the audience like me? Will my mind go blank when I start to speak? Have I prepared myself satisfactorily?

Always keep in mind that if the thought of conveying a speech makes you anxious, you are definitely not alone! Believe it or not, according to a regularly quoted survey, more people are afraid of public speaking than they are of dying. Those who have a high level of uneasiness while speaking are at a greater disadvantage than more conversational, self-confident individuals.

Folks who assertively express themselves are regarded as more capable. These folks also fashion a better impression during employment interviews and are more likely to be promoted than anxious individuals.

Confidence gives a positive impression and anxiety generates a negative one. When we speak, we are communicating in 3 different ways: verbally, visually, and vocally. Our verbal conveyance might be strong and well prepared; however, when we are anxious, the audience will very likely notice our negative vocal and visual signs, such as absence of eye contact, poor posture, timid delivery, and tense vocal quality. Nonetheless, when we are self-confident and our verbal, visual, and vocal indicators are in harmony, we will appear much more believable.

In order to have people trust us when we speak, and if we want to advance the impressions we make, we must learn to increase our confidence. The next chapter will offer you tips on how to manage any speech anxiety you may experience and teach you to be more confident and give professional deliveries.

Whatever you want to call it - anxiety, stage fright, or uneasiness, you must comprehend what it is for several reasons. First of all, anxiety can debilitate you. Secondly, misunderstandings about it can build up your anxiety. Lastly, knowing the strategies for handling speech anxiety can aid in lessening your nervousness.

Factors Contributing to Speech Anxiety

First of all, understand that speech anxiety is nothing new. It been around since the beginning of time. Speakers who have experienced speech anxiety recognize the significance of being calm and confident when speaking.

Some people continue to feel nervous, while others remain calm and relaxed. Issues in speech anxiety vary from person to person. But common issues relate to all of us.

Having knowledge of the causes of speech anxiety will be your initial step in handling it successfully. Various anxiety-generating issues affect virtually all of us, including:

- ✓ Poor Preparation
- ✓ Unsuitable Self-Expectations
- ✓ Fear of Assessment
- ✓ Extreme Self-Focusing
- ✓ Fear of the Audience
- ✓ Not Understanding our Body's Responses

Misconceptions about Speech Anxiety

No one believes speech anxiety is enjoyable. But, when we know why our bodies react as they do, we then become better equipped to face our anxieties.

Let's look at some misunderstandings and learn how to counter them.

Myth / Misconception	Reality
1. Everyone will know if a speaker has speech anxiety.	Few, if any, will notice. So keep the secret to yourself and start acting confident.
2. Speech anxiety will intensify as the speech progresses.	It's all up to you. Mostly, a well-prepared speaker will relax as the speech progresses.
3. Speech anxiety will ruin the effect of the speech.	If you let it, it will. On the contrary, speech anxiety may improve a speaker's effectiveness.
4. The audience is inherently hostile and will be overly critical of what we do.	Most listeners are polite especially when the speaker is obviously trying to do well.

Strategies for Managing Speech Anxiety

Each individual speaker should distinguish the different approaches offered for handling speech anxiety. Best of all, as you provide speeches, you will learn tactics that work particularly for you. Below are some strategies that have been extremely effective to countless speakers.

1. Be Well-Prepared and Practice Your Speech.

The one thing that can make you feel anxious prior to a speech is knowing that you are not well prepared. Seriously, isn't your anxiety about looking stupid in front of your audience? Poor preparation will pretty much guarantee this.

In order to get ready effectively, first you must attempt to know your listeners, if possible, and then shape your speech and visual aids for that precise group.

Then, you will arrange easy-to-follow notes. While using the notes, run through your speech 3 or more times from start to finish, speaking louder each time. Mentally going thru your speech is not at all the same thing as really talking in front of your audience. For example, if you are to be standing throughout your speech, stand while you are practicing. If you are going to use visual aids, practice using them also. And, as you practice, time yourself so you know if you should shorten or lengthen your speech.

Finally, anticipate potential questions and prepare answers. Knowing you are well prepared will help reduce so much of your anxiety.

2. Warm Up First.

Speakers are not any different from singers who warm up their voices, musicians who warm up their fingers, or athletes who warm up their muscles prior to a performance. Therefore, prior to giving a speech, you should warm up your voice and also loosen your muscles. Several methods can be done to help you do this.

Try singing up and down the scale, the same way singers do prior to their concert. Read a page from a book aloud, varying your volume, pitch, rate, and quality. Perform a few stretching exercises like touching your toes and rolling your head from side to side.

Warm-up exercises will assist you in relaxing and ensure that you are prepared to present at your best.

3. Use Deep Breathing.

One quick way to calm your nervousness is thru deep breathing. To do this, take in deep breaths thru your nose, and hold while counting to 5, then gradually exhale thru your mouth. As you are exhaling, imagine the stress and apprehension are gently slipping down thru your arms and then leaving out of your fingertips, and then going down your body and legs and finally out thru your toes. Repeat this procedure 2 or 3 times if needed.

4. Prepare an Introduction That Will Relax You and Your Audience.

More times than not, speakers learn that once they get an encouraging reaction from the audience, they relax instantly. Therefore, most speakers will begin with some type of humor. This helps to relax them and the audience. If a funny opening is not proper for the type of speech you are giving, or if you are just simply uncomfortable with humor, another alternative would be to share a personal experience. Whichever method you choose, make it work at the beginning so that you will feel more comfortable all through your speech.

5. Focus on Meaning.

Of importance is that rather than distressing about how you look or sound, or even about whether you are impressing your spectators, instead try to center your energy on getting your point across to the listeners. Be sure that your listeners are following the direction of your speech and comprehending your ideas. Instead of thinking about you, instead pay close attention to their nonverbal response. So, if you are noticing that they appear confused, explain your theory over again or maybe add an additional example. The speaker who focuses on their audience will quickly forget about being fearful.

6. Use Visual Aids.

Visual aids make listening more laid-back for the audience and also increases your confidence as the speaker. They also make it nearly impossible to overlook your key points. If you are unsure of your next point, just simply show your next visual aid. Furthermore, using visual aids like posters, flipcharts, or objects can add eye-catching actions to the presentation, and can also have you completely involved in your presentation, so you will be worried so much less by your appearance.

7. Develop a Positive Mental Attitude.

Using positive imagery, you will grow a positive, vibrant, and complete mental image of yourself. When you visualize yourself speaking confidently, you become more confident. You can pretend in your mind that you have feelings of pride, even when no real situation exists. Understandably, positive imagery alone won't give you the result you need without you preparing and practicing your speech.

Know that positive self-imagery can be used in various facets in your life. It can help you cope with nervousness during job interviews, problem-solving debates, testing conditions, or any situations in which your self-assurance requires a helping hand.

If you want to flourish in public speaking, you must envision yourself as an effective speaker. No extent of conversation, reassurance, or preparation will make you effective if you consider yourself a worried or unsuccessful speaker.

CHAPTER 5 - OVERCOMING YOUR FEAR

You must free yourself from 2 misconceptions:

1. Great speakers are born, and cannot be made. It is hopeless to attempt becoming one if you were not gifted with the God-given talent.
2. For almost all individuals, fear and nervousness can never be overcome. It is a waste of time to even try.

Here we take a look at each of these incorrect assumptions.

Are Good Speakers Born and Not Made?

I'd say that you don't really believe this, or you wouldn't even be reading through this book. We are all born as a baby, and babies cannot speak. Right? The "born speaker" myth is simply an excuse some use for not attempting at all. Those who say they believe it merely want to save face from the humiliation a bad speech could bring to them. It is a known fact that the old saying is true - "practice makes perfect".

When giving a speech, the speaker speaks to others for a given reason. You have truly been making speeches from the time you could talk. However, you didn't treat it then as the "dreaded speech."

You really can grow into a great speaker if you have and use these tools:

1. a voice
2. basic language skills: i.e., a working vocabulary and grammar
3. something to say
4. a need to express your ideas to others

You have, in fact, been using said tools for many years. You've been talking to others, a number of times every day, and you call it conversation. So, conversation is talking to a few people. Public speaking is, basically, the same, but talking to a bigger group.

Your audience is simply a crowd of individuals. You can chat effortlessly with 1 or 2 people, so just think of public speaking as talking to a few people all at the same time, or talking to the group as to one person.

Can You Conquer Fear?

There are 3 resolutions to aid you in reducing fear and making it work for rather than against you.

1. Take it as Mother Nature's method of helping you.

You do not need to be alarmed by fear. Be aware of it. Do not judge yourself for having it. We all have fear of one thing or another. Whether or not your fear comes from the thought of standing by yourself on a stage in front of hundreds of people, or from the thought of embarrassment when speaking, **keep in mind that you are reacting normally.**

Athletes are almost always anxious prior to a significant competition, musicians shudder prior to a concert, and performers have stage fright more often than not, even veteran performers. As a matter of fact, seasoned speakers never really lost their apprehension prior to speaking, nor do they want to.

An experienced actor once said: "*I used to have butterflies in my stomach every time I stand in front of an audience. Now that I know how to make them work for me, they fly in formation.*"

Now, knowing that you are experiencing a normal and common human reaction, you can get rid of the toughest aspect contributing to your fear. <u>You can quit judging yourself for being uncommon.</u>

Psychologists state that fear is not even the actual stumbling block. We feel uncomfortable or hopeless since we think that fear is wrong. It is not fear itself that is wrong, but rather our feelings about it that disappoints us.

How many times have we heard Franklin Roosevelt's note on the speech of Henry Thoreau: **"We have nothing to fear but fear itself."** This really sums it all up. The sooner you know this and become aware of it, you will be on your way to self-mastery.

Let's try to understand this. When you face a new or diverse situation, or when many eyes are watching you and you do not want to mess up, nature actually does something great to support you, but only if you recognize the help instead of being disappointed by it.

Learn to identify fear as your friend. Be aware of it, and use it well.

2. Analyze Your Fear.

Your next step in conquering fear is stress-free and painless. It is to evaluate your form of fear. As previously stated, fear is a tool for your protection. So, what are you protecting? You are concerned about your self-image. In public speaking, there are only 3 dangers to self-image:

(a) Fear of Yourself – Fear of poor performance or of not pleasing your self-image.

(b) Fear of Your Audience – Fear the audience might tease or laugh at you.

(c) Fear of Your Material – Fear that you have nothing practical to say or that you are not well-prepared.

(a) and (b) are very much connected. It is probable to please yourself and fail to please your audience. Targeting audience approval is most times a better alternative because, if you succeed, you are, in fact, also pleasing yourself.

Having said that, always remember that in seeking to satisfy the audience you must not ever compromise your message. There will be times when you might need to convey a message to individuals who you know are for the most part opposed to it. This instance calls for courage. Do not fear to disagree. Good speakers can and have done so and have proudly walked off the stage successfully. True beliefs prepare a speaker and can actually give great force to the speech.

3. Make use of what you have learned.

Now you know that fear, which is nature's secret defense, can essentially help you to succeed. You have learned that you are not actually afraid of fear but rather of yourself, your audience, and your material. Now, you can use this knowledge. And, here's how:

a. Hide undesirable outlooks from others. If you do not have much confidence, simply learn to hide it. Giving it away to the audience will not help at all. You should never discuss it. In fact, discussing it will just make you feel worse. In all circumstances, you need to act confident. It will really rub off on you, and you will end up looking the way that you are feeling.

Have you ever heard of the frightened boy who walked past the cemetery one dreary night? If he walked nonchalantly and whistled cheerfully, he was okay. However, when he walked fast, he could not reject the enticement to run. And then when he ran, the dread took over.

In other words, never give in. Remain cool and calm. Learn to enjoy your speech and your audience.

b. Evaluate your situation sensibly. Consider the reasons you were invited to speak. Know that amongst many other potential speakers, you were the one that was chosen. The person who requested you had confidence in you, or you would not have been chosen.

You are believed to be a capable speaker. And you obviously know a lot about the topic. In reality, you know more about it than your audience does.

Your valuation tells that you are equipped to do well and that you have the advantage over your audience. When you learn to accept this, your self-assurance will appear to your audience. It will make them trust in you and your speech.

c. Evaluate your audience rationally. You audience really wants you to do well. They actually suffer right along with a speaker who is having trouble delivering, and these people do not enjoy the speaker's anguish. So, basically you need to consider your audience as opposed to yourself. Gain their attention, and you will be much more confident, and all will be pleased.

d. Evaluate your material realistically. Dread of good material is the easiest one to overcome as the answer is simple: knowledge and preparation. Knowledge and preparation dismiss fear, but again, by themselves they do not automatically guarantee the conveyance of a successful speech.

The best start is to identify you do not need to be afraid – of yourself, of your audience, or of your material. And as you prosper in giving speeches, you will soon say, "I <u>can</u> do it because I <u>have</u> done it often."

PART TWO:

Preparing Your Speech

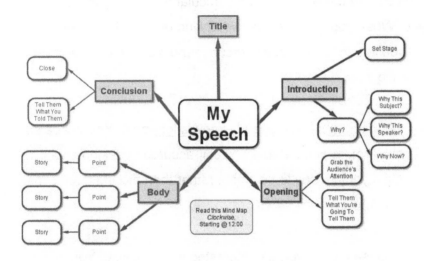

CHAPTER 6 - SELECTING YOUR TOPIC

In some cases, speakers are given a particular subject matter. However, most of the time, you will be given a broad kind of speech with the selection of a particular topic being left up to you. When you have decided what kind of speech you will be presenting, follow the below recommendations in choosing your specific topic:

- <u>Choose a topic you already know a lot about</u>. You will be so much more comfortable and self-assured speaking about a topic you already know about rather than picking a topic that you know nothing about.

- <u>Choose a topic you are interested in discussing</u>. You might know a decent amount about numerous subjects, but you might not be very interested in them. Don't choose these topics just because you know them. It is tough to interest your listeners in a topic that doesn't really interest you.

- <u>Choose a topic that you can make interesting and/or beneficial to your listeners</u>. Your audience may not necessarily be interested in your topic prior to your speech, but they should be interested by the time you are finished. If you evaluate your prospective audience, you will get a fairly good understanding of their interests.

- <u>Choose a topic that suits the requirements of the assignment</u>. It is important to know the sort of speech, the time limitations, and any other requirements, and select your subject matter as a result.

Ask yourself the following in order to come up with possible topics:

- ✓ What are my academic and enlightening interests?
    - ➢ What do I like to read?
    - ➢ What thought-provoking things have I learned from television?
    - ➢ What specific courses, or themes covered in courses, have especially interested me?

- ✓ What are my occupational objectives? What do I wish to do in life?

- ✓ What are my much-loved leisurely activities and interests? What do I do for fun that other people may be interested in learning more about?

- ✓ What are my own social concerns which are important to me?

> ➢ What is going on in my life which troubles or upsets me?

> ➢

> ➢ What is going on outside my life that seems unfair, unjust, or just in need of improvement?

Narrowing Down the Topic

Now you can chose your general topic and, you should be prepared to narrow it down on the foundation of your audience's interests and wants. Below are the steps to follow:

1. Select possible speech topics.

2. Reflect upon situational issues.
   ✓ Familiarity: Will my audience be familiar with any particular info which will assist me in selecting a topic?
   ✓ Current Events: Is there a topic to highlight current events which might be of substantial interest to my audience?
   ✓ Audience Apathy: Can I inspire the audience to be less indifferent to outlets that are thoroughly pertinent to me?
   ✓ Time Limits: Do I have enough time to discuss the topic adequately?

3. Reflect upon audience factors.
   - ✓ Previous Knowledge: What specifically do my listeners already know?
   - ✓ Common Experiences: What shared experiences have my listeners faced?
   - ✓ Common Interests: Where do my interests and my listeners' interests meet?
   - ✓ Relevant Diverse Factors: How different are my listeners?

4. Choice your Tentative Topic.

Some samples of thinning down can be seen below:

GENERAL TOPIC	NARROWED DOWN	NARROWED DOWN FURTHER	NARROWED DOWN EVEN FURTHER
Career Choices	career choices of graduates of top American schools	career choices of graduates of top American schools in the last 5 years	factors affecting the career choices of MBA graduates of Wharton School of Business in the last 5 years
Southeast Asia	security problems in	roots of terrorism in	cooperation among

43

	Southeast Asia	Southeast Asia	governments of Southeast Asia in addressing the problems of terrorism
Housing	housing projects in the last 10 years	housing projects in City X	financing problems in the housing projects in City X

Determining Your Exact Purpose

The elementary purpose of public speaking is to enlighten, teach, entertain, and influence. These 4 are not mutually exclusive of one another.

A speaker can have a number of purposes in mind. A couple might be to enlighten and entertain. Another speaker might want to enlighten but also at the same time persuade, motivate, or sway. Though content, organization, and conveyance may have 2 or more purposes, most have just one central purpose.

Speeches which inform offer correct statistics, impartial info, results, and sometimes, explanations of your results. Those that instruct teach the audience a method or procedure built on material delivered in the speech.

Those that entertain convey pleasure and enjoyment which causes your listener's to giggle. Speeches that persuade endeavor to sway the listener's to take an explicit stand on an issue.

Identifying the Objectives of the Speech

An objective is more partial and precise than a purpose. It could aim at a behavior or a thought. What does your message aim to accomplish? What response are you looking to get from the audience?

Does you wish to convince the audience to support a cause by joining a movement?

Do you want the audience to purchase a specific product or use a specific service?

Do you want the audience to change their behavior thru a process presented?

Do you want to inspire the audience to laugh and then later to reflect upon a pertinent social issue?

Do you want to deliver correct and trustworthy material in order to lead them to a decision?

As you receive answers to these questions, speech objectives can be recognized.

CHAPTER 7 - ANALYZING YOUR AUDIENCE

The more you are informed about your audience, the better you will be capable of connecting your topic to them. Audience study is not at all hard. It essentially necessitates knowing your audience well enough that you are able to organize your verbal, visual, and vocal delivery to fit their circumstances. When scrutinizing an audience, you are not attempting to betray, control, or have power over them; you are simply ensuring that your speech fits their needs and keeps them interested.

Speeches should be audience-centered. Thus, audience examination is a must. For true value, a speaker should learn the following:

1. Who does the audience consist of?

Do your best to take note of the over-all age, range, male/female percentage, educational background, profession, race, ethnic background, religion, geographic or ethnic background, political position, income level, memberships, etc.

2. What does your audience want from you?

Are they for a specific reason? Do they want you to explain current issues? Do they want to have fun? Do they require specific information? Has your audience attended on their own or were they required to attend?

Audiences who attend voluntarily are more likely to be similar and have the same things in common. Most involuntary audiences consist of students; they are diverse and vary in countless ways.

3. What is the size of your audience?

How big is the audience? Is it an audience of 10 or 100? In a classroom setting, you would probably be talking to approximately thirty or so students.

Audience size can sometimes attribute to our anxiety and can upset speech delivery. Generally, you want to speak more officially with the larger groups.

4. Where is the venue of your speech?

Will the venue be in a room? What kind of room will it be, a conference room, a hall, or a small meeting room?

When you present in a classroom, you are pretty much presenting in a familiar, relaxed setting. You tend to know if there is an overhead projector, whether the lights can be dimmed, etc.

As you present speeches, you will learn more about other settings, such as outdoor stages, or mall and hotel lounges. Try to learn about podiums, technological support, microphones, the sound system, etc.

Your audience investigation should obviously be done before the speech, though sometimes it happens during the speech itself. A thoughtful speaker can receive a good amount of info from the audience as the speech is being given. The hints are nonverbal, like alertness, facial expressions, edginess, nonparticipation, or boredom. When these signs are seen, you can be flexible and alter or adapt to do a better job.

Here is a model of audience analysis:

Topic: A Call for Support for Independence in Old Age
Purpose: To Influence
Objective/s: The presentation will look for pledges of effort, time, or money to help create an establishment to support independence in old age.

Audience Analysis:

1. Who are the listeners?	• Heads/officers of civic, religious and business communities in the city
	• Almost equal ratio of men and women who are professionals, with high educational attainments and high earning capacity, leaders in their specific fields, dominantly Christian audience with 65% Catholics, 85% married, American and American-Chinese, some Asians
	• Active in social and civic works
	• In touch with current political, social, and religious issues
	• In touch with prevailing business and government situations
2. What do they want from you?	• Basically interested in a topic that is relevant to their group or organization
	• Desire to get more information about dependency of old age, and to know more about what the speaker is going to propose/request

	• Want enough bases to decide whether or not to support • Came in response to a formal invitation
3. What is the size of the audience?	• 50 people
4. Where is the venue of the presentation?	• Medium-sized case room with fixed upholstered seats in a semi-circle • 2-ft elevation in the front for the speaker • Very good acoustics • Electronic devices for presentations

PART THREE:

Developing Your Speech

CHAPTER 8 - ORGANIZING YOUR SPEECH

Many speakers carefully choose their topics, choose a solid purpose, look for decent supportive resources, and nonetheless never have success in public speaking. It could be partially due to bad luck, but it is typically attributable to how they outlined and organized their thoughts.

It is kind of like writing an essay. You must begin with a thesis and choose the main points which will explain or cultivate it. Organizing, then, is stating the thesis of the speech and listing the key ideas that will be used to support it.

The Remember Box

Organizing the speech consists of 3 parts: the introduction, body, and conclusion. It is a thesis established with backing points. Speech indicators and transition devices tie the parts together.

Organizing the Introduction of Your Speech

The opening of your speech is vital. It gives your audience their initial impression of your topic, purpose, and chief point.

Nonetheless, your opening must do more than help them to appreciate your speech. It must also catch their interest. It is not enough to say, "Today I am going to talk about why the school needs a new basketball gym."

It is tough to attract the audience using this statement. The introduction needs to be better written so that your audience is inclined to listen closely and have some idea of your speech's objective.

A lot of good speeches end up falling short due to their puzzling and uninteresting introductions. If you do not get off to a good start, chances are your audience will tune you out. Keep in mind that just because people are a part of the audience does not mean that they plan to listen. This is why you should make it impossible for them not to.

Effective introduction comprises of seizing the attention of your audience immediately. When you first get up to speak, the audience will typically give you their complete attention. But that attention can be very short. Below are some means of keeping audience attention:

- ✓ Establish common ground. Audiences are much more probable to pay attention to speakers who they share common interests, problems, or goals.

✓ <u>A startling statement or statistic</u>. Use fascinating or astonishing statements or statistics which will provoke curiosity. For instance, "950,000 people in the Middle East may not be able to eat three meals a day in the year 2010." or "Dinosaurs aren't extinct. Every time you see a songbird, you're looking at a survivor from the Paleozoic era."

✓ <u>A story or a brief anecdote</u>. An exciting story, whether it is passionate, funny, perplexing, or captivating, directs attention. Your story can be factual or imagined. The story can be a personal experience, or it can be something you have read. For instance, "An interesting thing happened on my way here today." or "The first time I jumped out of a plane..."

✓ <u>A pretentious or actual question</u>. Pretentious questions do not require immediate answers. They are simply meant to prompt the audience to think about an issue or concept.

✓ <u>A quote</u>. You can use the words of a well-known author, a performer, a singer, athlete or any other famous and greatly respected figures to get the audience's interest and attention.

✓ <u>Use humor</u>. Speakers will often begin a speech with a funny story. However, irrespective of how funny a story is, it should be suitable to the point you are trying to make. Simply telling a few jokes is not a good way to announce a speech, and a joke that falls flat is embarrassing. Humor should never be impolite and should never be intended to mock someone or something, so you must be extremely cautious.

You can use more than a few of the above at the same time. For example, you could tell an exciting story that also creates common ground and piques interest.

Pausing right after telling a captivating story, asking a rhetorical question, or sharing an unforgettable quote can help the listeners to reflect upon what you are about to speak about. Whichever technique you use, make sure it attracts in the way in which a magnet attracts. The vital dynamic here is seizing and keeping the listeners' curiosity and attention.

An effective introduction catches attention and creates audience interest on the topic. It also generates suitable expectations by preparing the audience to get the message. So, what 3 individual parts make up the introduction?

a) <u>The Opening</u> – This is your first sentence. It can be a quote, a surprising statement or statistic, or a brief story. The opening should be short, thought-provoking, and fitting to the topic.

b) The Topic – This is merely declaring the title of your speech. Say it directly such as: "I have been asked to speak about _____." or "I have chosen to speak to you about _____."

c) The Agenda – This briefly describes your points of view or what you will be discussing.

Here is an example of an introduction:

(1) Good afternoon everybody. (2) It is a pleasure to be here with you today. (3) I have been asked to introduce myself and I've been given 3 minutes. (4) There is not much I can tell you about myself in that length of time. So, what I will do in its place is begin with my topic which is **The Increasing Involvement of Women in Social Issues Today**. (5) I feel very intensely that women's reaction to present social issues are apparent in, one, the way she deals with home and family life, two, her contribution or backing of community-based groups for change, and three, her participation in national issues over a tougher sense of mindfulness of these matters.

Sentences 1-3 are the openers, sentence 4 is the topic and sentence 5 is the agenda.

The introduction is short, straight-forward, and will capture the audience's attention while getting them ready for what is to come. In a thought-provoking manner, an introduction unmistakably forms the topic and sets a guide on what the listeners can expect from your speech.

Organizing the Body of Your Speech

At this point in time, you are ready to establish your chief ideas and deliver visual and verbal supports. The body of your speech is the meat, and you should produce the key points you want to develop in this part of the speech. These key points should be simple, declarative sentences so they will be simply recognized and remembered by the people who heard your speech. These points require backing, explanation, interpretation, and data. They can be the form of explicit and solid details, contrasts, illustrations, and graphics.

There are many steps you can do to make your key points unforgettable:

1. Limit yourself to no more than 3 to 5 key points.
2. Keep your key points short and use corresponding configurations when possible.
3. Position your material so that you cover your most vital point either first or last.

4. Make your key points unforgettable by fashioning your own rhyme or short form when possible.

Organizing the Conclusion of Your Speech

Many speakers do not really conclude their speeches. They simply stop talking.

The conclusion is very important. It slowly guides the audience back to an inclusive valuation of the discussion. Of course, a knowledgeable discussion in the body will give the speaker more freedom to maneuver a conclusion.

No speech is thorough without a closing remark because the conclusion confirms all concepts were implicit and remembered. It provides the desirable ending. It is likely that some may have missed, misunderstood, or forgotten a point. Without a conclusion, you can't correct these glitches. A conclusion is also crucial due to the fact that the audience likes and needs that closure.

Conclusion is predominantly substantial if you have a question-and-answer period at the end of your speech. Offer a brief summary prior to the question-and-answer and another one after it to tie up loose ends and redirect attention back to the key points presented.

As in the beginning, the ending should be fairly brief, if at all possible not more than 1/7 of the entire speech. The smaller you make your ending, the more powerful it will appear to your audience, and the more effortlessly they will remember it.

Below are some practices to make effective conclusions:

1. Recap what you told the audience – your key points and thoughts.
2. Issue a challenge to the audience.
3. Make a plea to the audience for action.
4. Envision the future.
5. Include unforgettable quotes.
6. Mention the introduction - return the audience to your opening statement.

Because conclusions are so important and possibly unforgettable, they should (1) be as short as possible, (2) by no means ramble, (3) never present new info, and (4) be created cautiously. Now you know, the conclusion of your speech is too essential to take lightly. If you style your conclusion cautiously, you will close your speech with a tactical close and yield a finishing positive result.

If you find that your time is getting low, do not get rid of your conclusion. It is better to condense your final ideas than to eliminate the conclusion. If you practice timing your speech, you will not even have to be worried about time.

CHAPTER 9 - OUTLINING YOUR SPEECH

How do you feel when you hear the word outline? If you have a terrible feeling about it, maybe you have never truly learned how to outline correctly, or perhaps your prior experiences with the outline have not been good. Whatsoever the reason, trust that you are not alone. Many people dislike outlining. This is actually unfortunate since, when done correctly, they can save you a lot of time and help you progress a great deal.

Basic Principles of Outlining

The outline will not only benefit you in seeing the over-all idea of your speech. In addition, it will aid you in subdividing the body of your message into sub-topics according to the order of their importance.

The outline always helps.

I. So, what is an outline?
   A. An outline is basically note-taking displaying how your ideas.
   B. It also displays how your ideas are linked to one another.

II. What steps should you follow when outlining?

    A. Attempt to learn the most vital idea or the key idea.

        1. This will be your title or thesis statement.

        2. Think in precise terms when doing your outline.

    B. Look for great ways to improve or split up the key point. This will give you the most important headings of your outline. Contemplate gestures or transition words to specify:

        1. Sequential Order

        2. Details

        3. Cause and Effect Relationships

        4. Basic to Detailed/Easy to Hard

        5. Compare-Contrast

    C. Attempt to Stress Details.

        1. Stress what you believe is vital or complex and requires a thorough description.

        2. Each time, attempt to associate these details with your major points.

III. Notation In Outlining

    A. The magnitude of the indentation and the notation used are determined by the significance of your idea.

1. The most significant or main ideas are positioned to the farthermost left and are noted with roman numerals (I, II, III).
2. The following most significant ideas are positioned under the main ideas and are given capital letters (A, B, C).
3. The minor details are positioned to the right under the main details and are given plain numbers (1, 2, 3).

B. All of your ideas of equal significance should have the same indentation, with all main ideas being allocated with roman numerals and being furthest to the left.

C. You can write items in an outline as either phrases or sentences, but the full outline should be one or the other. So basically, do not mix phrases and sentences in the same outline.

D. At all times, capitalize the first word of every item in your outline.

E. Always put a period after each notation symbol in your outline.

IV. What are the advantages of having an Outline?

A. It is easier to recognize potential problems.

B. It is less challenging to ask for workable assessments.

C. There is less enticement to remember your
    speech.

D. Flexibility is improved.

See below for an example.

Pat Smart

English 111-77b

Professor Donna Reiss

May 12, 2000

No More Traffic Jams on I-64:

Mass Transit for South Hampton Roads

Thesis statement: Instead of further road construction, which will only increase the amount of
traffic in South Hampton Roads, the cities of Norfolk, Portsmouth, Chesapeake, and Virginia
Beach should develop a modern mass transit system of light rail and park-and-ride express buses.

I.   Current traffic problems
     A.   Morning rush
     B.   Afternoon rush
II. Proposed solutions
     A.   More highways and lanes
          (1)   Virginia Department of Transportation
          (2)   City of Norfolk
          (3)   City of Portsmouth
     B.   Light rail
          (1)   City of Virginia Beach
                (a)   City Council
                (b)   Citizens for Rapid Transit
                (c)   Environmental Protection Agency
          (2)   City of Norfolk

PART FOUR:

Presenting Your Speech

CHAPTER 10 - PREPARING YOUR VISUAL AIDS EFFECTIVELY

One of the best means to guarantee a popular and effective speech is to use attention-grabbing and commanding visual aids. Regrettably, many public speakers either do not use visual aids at all or use overloaded, difficult-to-read visuals which makes it nearly impossible for the audience to comprehend the visuals' content, to listen to the speech, and to take down notes at all.

Below par visual aids require your audience to choose between listening to you and just reading the visual aid to understand. Hence, when formulating the visuals, keep in mind that if your audience is going to take longer than about 7 seconds to grasp the content, they will probably fall into a reading mode. When your listeners are flung into reading mode, they hear practically nothing you are actually saying.

Audiovisual aids can be used to strengthen, clarify, or further explain the key points. These aids consist of graphs, flipcharts, slides, videotapes, etc. Communication success is often heightened by the use of more than one aid. So, when you opt to use visual aids, you should present the relevance of their use to your message.

Functions of Visual Aids

Visual aids, when used successfully, can assist a speaker with communicating better and can also assist the listeners in understanding better. Visual aids employ the senses and help to explain, support, and support the message. Visual aids are so effective that almost all speakers use them.

Let's talk about the ways visual aids can improve your presentation. They can:

✓ offer support and highlight key ideas
✓ enable understanding
✓ inspire emotional connection
✓ help with delivery
✓ add to your believability
✓ lessen your anxiety since they provide you something to do with your hands, they pull audience attention away from you, and make it nearly impossible to overlook what you are saying.

The audience also profits from the active use of visual aids. These aids can:
• help separate significant from less significant info
• add curiosity and color
• develop audience memory

CHAPTER 11 - DELIVERING YOUR MESSAGE EFFECTIVELY

With all the planning that you have put into your speech, you ultimately are ready to present it to the audience. You probably have spent a lot of time analyzing your prospective audience, selecting your topic, and organizing and rehearsing your speech. The actual delivery is the highpoint and climax of your public speaking experience.

Conveyance is one of the most apparent parts of public speaking, the part which entices the primary attention of both the speaker and the audience.

Clearly, delivery is not everything. A great delivery will not compensate for a poorly organized message, or one demanding substance. However, we realize the importance of delivery, yet at times it still panics us. You probably feel pretty comfortable arranging the speech, conducting the research, forming and outlining your ideas. Still, when confronted with the real delivering, the nerves start kicking in. Therefore, the more we learn about delivery, the better our chances of completing it magnificently. It is the obvious and important part.

Take for instance, Oprah Winfrey. How does she do it? She is passionate, motivating, influential, convincing, compassionate, and, most significant of all, authentic. She recognizes how to bond with her audience by connecting with them verbally, visually, and vocally. And so can you!

In order to make your presentation believable, always remember to get lots of practice.

Visual Delivery

Since the initial imprint comes more from what the audience sees than what they hear, we will now talk about visual delivery, mainly, how you appear to the audience. As a speaker, your physical presence, posture, facial expressions, eye contact, body movements, and gestures all effect your listeners' opinion.

The audience judges your appearance as a clue to your position, reliability, and awareness of the subject. Your safest bet is to always dress conservatively.

Good posture is simply standing straight and having your chest out and stomach in. Good posture makes the speaker appear and feel comfortable, and also helps voice projection and composure.

Move around sporadically. Body movement can add attentiveness, liveliness, and sureness to your presentation. To add emphasis, attempt moving at the start of an idea or at a transition between ideas

Gestures are movements of the hands, arms, head, and shoulders to help you communicate. They play an important part in speaking, nonetheless they need to increase communication and not encumber it. Make gestures when rehearsing your speech. Practice in front of a mirror, even to the point of overstating. Then adjust your gestures to a point where they are fitting and natural. Nevertheless, gestures should be spur-of-the-moment. Too many gestures could sidetrack your audience.

One kind of gesture is facial expression. This discloses your attitudes and feelings. Either choose to let your face glow with joy or burn with passion. Avoid the poker face, which will reveal nothing.

Eye contact is an extremely important aspect in getting and holding their attention. Look at your listeners directly, not above them or at the floor or ceiling or out of the window; or else, you lose your contact.

Here are some questions you might consider:
- ✓ Do I gesture enough? Or, too much?
- ✓ Does my body movement strengthen the course of my speech?
- ✓ Are my gestures troubling?

✓ Am I depending on any one gesture too much?

✓ Does my face express the importance or sentiment I am attempting to convey?

✓ Are there any other gestures, body movements, or facial expressions that could show my envisioned meaning more efficiently?

Vocal Delivery

Voice is crucial in communication; only through voice can any speech conveyance be accomplished successfully.

An effective voice is informal, natural, and passionate. The audience will listen better if you speak as you do in a normal conversation.

Sounds have 4 essential characteristics: volume, pitch, rate, and quality. If any of these is defective, distraction results.

1. Volume

A well-modulated voice is vital to being an effective speaker. Many individuals have very soft voices. Those with soft voices while speaking can often be viewed as dull. A person who wants to cultivate an attractive, beautiful, and energetic personality should undertake training in voice projection.

If you are speaking to a group, each and every member of the audience with normal hearing and concentration should be able to comprehend your statements without straining their ears and without getting annoyed because of an unreasonably loud voice.

An important standard in speaking clearly is that consonants should be pronounced well. Vowels are easier to pronounce, yet consonants give lucidity to speech.

A voice that is controlled by intellect rather than passion tends to be moderate in pitch as well as in loudness. This does not suggest that intellectual efforts are empty of feeling. It just suggests that intellectual efforts complemented by vocalization are not usually branded by the overstated range and intensity of feeling displayed in emotional behavior alone.

2. Pitch

Pitch is the common level on a musical scale of the voice in speech. If a person is consistently edgy, the voice is frequently in a greater pitch level than that of a consistently calm individual. Pitch may be high, medium, or low, or soprano, alto, baritone, or bass for vocal pitch.

Natural pitch in speaking is significant for an effective voice. Someone who speaks unnaturally will be unsuccessful, displeasing, and uncomfortable.

3. Rate

There are 3 rates or tempos in speaking – slow, average, and fast. A distinctly slow speaking rate shows somberness, grief, or sadness. A noticeable upsurge in rate is indicative of cheerfulness, enjoyment, delight, or anger. Words or phrases that are spoken more slowly and more forcefully are considered more important and more intellectually noteworthy than quickly pronounced words. Though, a constant, fixed rate of speech is discouraged irrespective of feeling, mood, or purpose because it is dull.

Fluctuations in rate can be attained by the rate of enunciation or by the use of pauses. The use of pauses is a very valuable method for separating or grouping phrases, for producing intense effects, and for highlighting ideas. As an over-all rule, the use of a comma is a sign for the reader or speaker to pause. But in some cases, long sentences without commas should also be separated according to thought content by a pause to give time for breathing and for the audience to comprehend fully what is being read or said.

Dramatic effect can be attained by speakers who pause after a growing articulation, thus generating suspense, after which the anticipated outcome follows to the gratification of the audience. Effective speakers, though, ought to elude pauses displaying

74

that they do not know what to say next. Speakers who know how to pause with intent and without distress are esteemed speakers.

4. Quality

Voice characteristics, or voice timbre, and voice attitudes, or voice color, fall under the common term of voice quality. An individual's voice can be characterized as pleasant or unpleasant contingent upon its timbre and color or quality.

So, what is voice quality? This term is tough to classify and no effort will be made to define it apart from showing its relationships to other aspects and how to achieve this. Vocal quality is connected to timbre and to the circumvention of unwanted vocal characteristics such as extreme nasality and breathing. It is also linked to feeling and mood.

Verbal Delivery

In addition, being really aware of your visual delivery and vocal delivery, your listeners will focus on your verbal delivery. The audience prefers speakers who use a more relaxed language than what is typical for written reports. For example, in oral speech, it is more suitable to use short, simple sentences, and it is not always necessary to use complete sentences.

Furthermore, it is unquestionably satisfactory to use personal pronouns such as I, we, you, and us and contractions such as I'm and don't, forms that are often eluded in formal written reports.

A mistake sometimes made is to use long or enormously technical terms or verbiage to amaze the audience. Although you are talking in a professional situation, do not think that your audience uses or understands the same technical words or verbiage that you do. The greatest language is vibrant and intriguing, solid and precise, and humble.

Putting your ideas into simple, easy-to-understand language that fits the circumstances of the listeners and is vibrant, precise, and bias-free can be trying at the start. But, as you practice on the basics of delivery and recollect the rules discussed, your language and style of speaking will definitely progress.

Methods of Delivery

There are 4 means of conveying a speech: impromptu, manuscript reading, memorization, and extemporaneous.

1. The Impromptu Speech

Of the 4 methods, the impromptu speech needs the smallest amount of groundwork. With very little advance notice, you are requested to speak for a few minutes on a particular subject. Attempt to apply the following principles or procedures in presenting a spur-of-the-moment speech.

1. Articulate the chief idea. Do not attempt to discuss the full issue. Limit yourself to a particular part that you can discuss within a few minutes. Make sure that you know the idea you wish to present prior to starting.
2. Begin your speech with a sentence which really says something. Do not be apologetic. Start with a bang, and go right to the point.
3. The body of the speech needs to be unified. You may provide illustrations, diagrams, comparisons, and contrasts to assist you in explaining your main sentences. Be as solid and precise as possible.
4. Close on a solid note. You can repeat your main sentences, but rearticulate them. Restate them concisely but clearly.

Below are some more recommendations relative to giving a spur-of-the-moment speech:

- ✓ Anticipate the likelihood that you might be called on to speak, so prepare early.
- ✓ Make the most of whatever slight amount of preparation time you are given to your advantage.
- ✓ Practice active listening.
- ✓ Manage speech apprehension by reminding yourself that nobody anticipates you to be flawless when you are asked to give spur-of-the-moment speeches.
- ✓ Use the essential principles of speech organization.
- ✓ Ponder the spur-of-the-moment speech as a golden opportunity to practice and improve your delivery.

2. The Manuscript Speech

A manuscript or read speech is a speech which is written and read word-for-word throughout. When the instance is a solemn or momentous one, the read speech is the most fitting. Individuals of distinction read their speeches for accurateness and correctness. This kind of speech is absent of naturalness and genuineness that the spur-of-the-moment speech or the impromptu speech has. The speaker reading the speech needs to keep a connection with the audience.

Below are some recommendations in giving a manuscript speech:

- ✓ Use a manuscript for the correct reasons.
- ✓ Use decent oral style.
- ✓ Practice intensively.
- ✓ Look for chances to move and gesture.
- ✓ Use your voice efficiently.
- ✓ Stay flexible.

3. The Memorized Speech

This technique of delivery is good only for diction pieces. The same as the read speech, it lacks naturalness and spontaneity. In addition, human memory may fail the speaker in the course of the delivery and can cause humiliation. This type of speech should not be used in public speaking classes.

Below are a few recommendations in presenting a memorized speech:

- ✓ Remain focused on your exact purpose and on the main ideas you want to deliver.
- ✓ Speak in the moment.
- ✓ Practice, practice, practice!

4. The Extemporaneous Speech

This technique is suggested for public speaking classes. It is not read or memorized. It has naturalness and spontaneity. In addition, the speaker has time to arrange the ideas personified in it, and yet the language is expressed at the moment of delivery.

This speech is also practiced but the words and organization of words are altered to something better and more effective. In practicing, the speaker is merely directed by a mental outline. If notes are used, they only contain quotes from famous authors and speakers which will help develop their ideas. The speaker does not remember the speech but knows from memory the order of ideas to attain harmony, organization, and clearness in speech.

An extemporaneous speech:
- ✓ Necessitates preparation.
- ✓ Is founded on a key-word outline.
- ✓ Permits the speaker to stay direct, involved, and flexible.

Practicing Your Speech

Sometimes, speakers read through the outline silently a couple of times and think they are all set. No true. If you do not practice your speech out loud more than a few times, more than likely you are not ready to speak.

There is a big difference between reading about how to provide an effective speech and really doing it. The only way to translate what you have read into what you can do is to practice. Remember that your objective is to sound poised and be natural. If you have been visualizing yourself giving a fruitful speech, you have taken a vital initial move to confident delivery. Good or bad speeches are a matter of practice. Habits are shaped and established thru continuous practice.

Feeling self-confident while talking is one of the rewards of practicing. The greatest results are realized if you prepare in 2 ways:

1. By visualizing yourself giving an effective and fruitful speech, and,
2. By really practicing your speech out loud.

These are some pointers when practicing your speech.

✓ First, read thru your speech silently more than a few times until you are prepared to start. Nevertheless, doing this isn't practicing speech delivery. It might help you to find glitches in your organization and might help you acquaint yourself with your material, but it will not help with your vocal and visual delivery and will only help a bit with your verbal delivery.

✓ Practice providing your speech out loud with your notes and outline. There is no substitute for practicing out loud on your feet, by means of your notes and visual aids, practicing your gestures and eye contact, and speaking out loud.

✓ Stand straight in front of a full-length mirror positioned at a distance where your audience would potentially be.

✓ For your initial rehearsals, use your outline until you are sure of your key points and their order.

✓ After the initial rehearsal, pause and ask yourself if the order you followed is the greatest order of ideas conceivable, if the material you collected is enough, if the way you articulated your ideas is the finest, and if your choice of words is suitable.

✓ Practice your speech out loud all the way thru, noticing portions that are bumpy, revisiting your notes, and practicing again.

✓ Distribute the speech into portions and practice main segments, like the introduction, numerous times recurrently.

✓ Recap the practice session as many times as required until you have increased your self-confidence and self-assurance, taking note of the correct enunciation and pronunciation of your vowels and consonants, proper pausing and phrasing, stress, optimum pitch, and volume.

✓ When you are rationally sure of your main headings and subtopics and their order, you can set aside your outline and practice with only your notes.

✓ Each time take a break. Elude practicing so much at one time that you start to lose your energy, voice, or concentration.

✓ Practice without help at first. Record your speech and play it back to get a reaction on your vocal delivery. Avoid dissecting your delivery. Focus on chief concerns.

✓ When possible, visit the room where you will speak and practice using the equipment or practice in a room comparable to the one in which you will be speaking. If your practice room does not have the equipment required for using your visuals, act out handling them. If you are presenting a manuscript speech, be sure that the manuscript is double or triple spaced in 14 or 16-point type. Put manuscript pages into a sturdy binder. Practice holding the binder high enough that you can gaze down at the manuscript without having to bob your head.

✓ When you start to feel comfortable with your speech, practice in front of a small audience (friends or family members). Ask them for detailed comments and feedback on your verbal, visual, and vocal delivery. Practice making direct eye contact and using gestures. If you have a video camera, let someone film you so that you can see yourself. If you see any awkward spots in your speech, decide how to adjust the speech to smooth them out.

✓ Practice your speech over again numerous times, all the way thru, but guard against memorization. Note that practice does not mean memorize.

✓ Be sure to time yourself a number of times. If your speech is too long, make proper cuts. For instance, you might cut a portion that is less significant, use fewer graphics, revise long quotes, or inform the audience that you will be happy to address a topic more fully during the question-and-answer period. Note that, if your speech is too long or too short, you may disrupt the audience's anticipations and damage your reliability.

✓ At least once prior to the real speech, practice using your visual aids with all the required equipment. Videotape yourself if possible, or ask a friend to watch one of your final practices.

✓ Get enough sleep the night before. On the day of the speech, get to the location early so that you can compose yourself. Check to see that your notes and visuals are in the correct order, and read through your outline one last time.

Keep in mind that no-one expects you to be perfect. If you make a mistake, correct it if necessary and continue. Then forget it. If you have practiced until you feel comfortable with your speech and have imagined yourself giving an effective speech, you should feel excited and self-assured.

Response to Audience Questions

The key to effective question-and-answer times is to truly be acquainted with your topic and anticipate questions from the audience. One of the most exasperating things about speaking is having to exclude so much vital material from your speech due to time limits. Nonetheless, if you are preparing a question-and-answer period to go with your speech, it is nearly impossible to know everything about your topic. The more you know, the better your answers will be.

Aside from knowing your topic, anticipate numerous questions that you think your audience might ask and prepare one or two visual aids to use when answering these questions. Before preparing completely new visuals, check to see if one or more overlays can be built-in to a visual that you want to use in your speech. The overlays would be used only during the question-and-answer period.

Surely, it's always probable that none of these questions will be asked. But just in case, you can affect your audience immensely. The subsequent recommendations might help you with your question-and-answer period. If you conduct audience questions well, you can make your message more resounding.

- ✓ Listen considerately to each question asked.
- ✓ If suitable, repeat the question before answering it so that everyone can hear it and keep track of what is going on.
- ✓ Rearticulate any perplexing or negative questions in a clear and positive way.
- ✓ Think a minute before answering each question. If you don't know the answer, say so, and refer the asker to someone in the audience who does know. Or, tell the person that it's a good question and that you will find the answer and let that person know in the next meeting.
- ✓ Do not allow one person to take over the forum period.
- ✓ If you think a question is unrelated or will take too long to answer, thank the person for the question and mention

that you will talk with that individual personally about it after the period.

✓ Do not try to fake your way thru a reply.

✓ Do not debate or get irritated or defensive while answering questions. What you say during the question-and-answer period will affect the audience's overall judgment of your reliability and your speech.

✓ If applicable, aggressively inspire listeners to contribute.

✓ If you anticipate an argumentative audience, avoid a question-and-answer period in any way possible. If not, mention in your introduction that there will be a short question-and-answer period at the end of your speech and ask the audience to write out questions during the speech. After your initial conclusion, collect the questions, select 3 or 4 good ones, and answer them – disregarding the less desirable ones.

✓ Watch your time, and end the period with a final conclusion that refocuses audience attention and puts a pleasing closure on your speech.

CHAPTER 12 - FINAL QUESTIONS

Q: How do I manage fear, apprehension, stage fright, and speech anxiety?

A: Gradually. These are very usual situations even for experienced speakers. Increased nervousness and rapid heartbeat before a speech are the coping mechanisms of the body. The more experienced you become, the better prepared you will be. Every one of us experiences this so it is good to breathe out the accumulated carbon dioxide in your lungs and breathe deeply before you begin your speech. Beginning your speech slowly helps decrease nervousness.

Q: How do I capture and maintain the listener's attention and interest?

A: Remember the following:
- ✓ Establish eye contact with the audience.
- ✓ Do not talk if someone is walking down the aisle or if there is audience movement.
- ✓ Make appropriate pauses for the audience to catch their breath.
- ✓ Use interesting and powerful visual aids.
- ✓ Talk from personal experience and tell stories.
- ✓ Make your speech concise.

Q: How do I know when the listeners are bored and inattentive?

A: Observe the following:

✓ A lot of listeners sit with their arms folded.

✓ Vacant looks – no smiles or nodding of the head.

✓ People are yawning.

✓ Polite coughs.

✓ Nonverbal signs. People are frequently looking at their watches, shuffling their feet, and worse starting to exit the building.

Q: How do I develop my self-confidence?

A: Practice. Practice is the key. Look for every chance to give a speech. The more you face the audience, the more you will develop self-confidence. Begin with very short speeches that last three to four minutes. Always bear in mind that a short speech can barely go wrong. Impromptu speeches make good practice. Concentrate and be natural. Do not try to pretend to be someone else. Master your topic. Believe in yourself. If you don't, no one else will.

Q: How much information must I gather for a speech?

A: Your experience is your guide. Some need 60 minutes of information for a 5-minute speech. You will have to read widely. At times you have to conduct some research. The most important information is your personal experience.

Q: Can I memorize a speech?

A: Yes, you can. But don't. Never memorize a speech. You are bound to miss out a line or two and worse, your speech will likely be insincere. Your listeners will discover anyway. Memorizing stops you from being natural. If you like, you may memorize a specific poem or a memorable quote.

Q: Can I read a speech?

A: Yes, you can. But don't. That is the best technique to bore a listener. The only instance you read a speech is when you do it on behalf of someone else. Even when you do that, make it brief or summarize it. At the end of the summary, give out the entire speech in the form of a handout. The written language and the spoken language are different forms of expression. What is beautifully written may not sound beautiful when it is spoken.

Q: Can I use notes during a speech?

A: Yes, you can. But be sure that they don't appear bulky. The worst thing a speaker can do is to pull out pages and pages of notes before a speech. Preparing 3" x 5" index cards is all right. Be sure your entire speech does not go beyond seven cards. A single sheet of paper with an outline of your speech is still the best. Be sure the letters on that single sheet are big enough to read.

Q: How do I develop my speech?

A: Never talk about one idea too long. If you have three ideas, allot equal time to each. The transition from one idea to the next must be smooth. Listeners must not wait too long for the next idea.

Q: During an open forum, what do I do when a person gives a speech rather than a question?

A: It is your responsibility to interrupt and say, "Excuse me, what exactly is your question?"

Q: What do I do when I get a hostile question?

A: Be cool. Be courteous and disagree with a smile by saying, "Perhaps I was not clear." or "It's possible you misunderstood."

Q: What do I do when someone has many questions in one question?

A: Answer them one by one and begin with the easiest.

And lastly…
Take time out to listen to as many speeches as possible. A good listener is a successful communicator. Don't forget to take down notes when you listen to these speeches.
Recognize speeches that you like and those you can't stand. Examine the speeches you like, and there you will learn useful and helpful tips to develop your speech. Examine the speeches you dislike, and there you will learn what you should prevent. Communication is as greatly a manner of listening as it is of speaking.

Printed in the USA
CPSIA information can be obtained
at www.ICGtesting.com
LVHW061127170823
755276LV00003B/472